Transformed
by
Trust

Transformed by Trust

by

Trust

From Questioning to Confident

ELAINE MARIE BARTON

Published by Redemption Press Express, PO Box 427, Enumclaw, WA 98022, (360) 226-3488.

Redemption Press Express is honored to present this title in partnership with the author. The views expressed or implied in this work are those of the author. Redemption Press Express provides our imprint seal representing design excellence, creative content, and high-quality production.

All Scripture quotations are taken from THE HOLY BIBLE, NEW INTERNATIONAL VERSION®, NIV® Copyright © 1973, 1978, 1984, 2011 by Biblica, Inc.® Used by permission. All rights reserved worldwide.

ISBN 13 : 978-1-64645-018-3 (paperback)
978-1-68314-955-2 (hardcover)
978-1-64645-162-3 (ePUB)

Library of Congress Catalog Card Number : 2023912094

Contents

*May the God of hope fill you with all joy and peace
as you trust in him, so that you may overflow with
hope by the power of the Holy Spirit.*

ROMANS 15:13

CHAPTER 1

What is this book about, and why should I read it?

I was born on the night of the Academy Awards in 1983. If I had won, I would have made the following acceptance speech:

> I'd like to thank my mom for making me go to church every Sunday. I'd like to thank every Sunday school and vacation Bible school teacher who told me Jesus loves me. Thanks to the pastors, especially Kevin, Barry, Steve, and Forest, and the small-group leaders, conference speakers, and authors who have shared their wisdom and insights with me. And a special shout-out to my Bible study friends, past and present, because not a single idea in this book is original. I'm simply putting together many truths I've discovered about living with Jesus and attempting to combine them into something coherent and useful.

For the first thirteen years of my life, I learned about Jesus, Noah, Moses, David, the good Samaritan, and other Bible characters—all made of felt. I sang a lot of songs and made crafts with crosses on them. I believed in God and heaven and angels. As a reward for memorizing the names of the first twenty books of the Bible, I got an ice cream sundae. I tried to be good most of the time, but that was hard because I had a younger brother.

As a teenager, I began to wonder if I was missing something. I still believed in God, but there was a lot about Him that I didn't understand. I particularly wondered, if Jesus was living in me, why couldn't I feel Him? I also noticed that, although I wanted to be a good person, I didn't always want to do good things. Especially when my brother reached top annoyance levels.

I did all my chores but sometimes felt grumpy about it. I didn't remember any Bible characters being grumpy, so I thought Christians were supposed to always feel happy. Now I know that these are issues all Christians have to face at some point, but at that time I assumed I was the only one. I accepted Jesus as Lord four times because I was never sure I'd done it right. I really wanted Jesus to change me, but I never felt anything change.

My junior year of high school, I started to feel sick often and had trouble sleeping. I was diagnosed with depression. I didn't feel sad; my body and my brain just didn't always work well together. I had friends, but not any of the popular kids. I did not care at all about fitting in. I became apathetic about my grades. I did pretty well in the classes I enjoyed, like English, but I basically gave up on chemistry. Medication helped me eat and sleep better, but I still had this strange feeling that I wasn't myself.

A few months after I started the medication, my boyfriend broke up with me, and a week after that, a close friend died in a car accident. Everything in the world seemed dark and meaningless. I felt empty. Activities I used to love no longer brought me happiness.

I knew my friends also were grieving, but I didn't see them suffering in the same way I did, and we didn't talk about it much. I prayed a lot and asked God to take away my pain and help me feel like myself again. That I survived through the rest of high school is literally a miracle.

After graduation, I went to college. I attended a different church and Bible study and met new people, including a friend I later married. I saw that I could go on, and I even had hope for good things in it. I thanked God that life was getting better. I spent more time reading the Bible and praying than I ever had before.

But the questions I'd had before hadn't been answered clearly. I was still certain there was a God, but I didn't know how to reconcile His powerful love with the bad things that happened to good people. I didn't understand why, if God sent Jesus to save us, He still let some people go to hell. At my state university, I was exposed to people with various worldviews, which added to my confusion.

I went through a rebellious period, during which I stopped going to church and reading the Bible. I read books about other religions, but none of them made any more sense to me than Christianity. I once told someone, "I'm a spiritual person. I'm just not religious." I thought I knew what would be good for me better than God did. To be honest, part of me just wanted to fit in with my college friends and make some questionable choices without much guilt.

I didn't do anything really horrible or scandalous. (At least none of my friends would have been scandalized, though maybe my grandmother would.) Looking back, it's obvious God was always with me, because I didn't suffer many consequences I could have incurred from my choices.[1]

---

1   I do not think that God spares believers from all consequences of their actions. I only believe that His plan for me did not include them at that time. In chapter 3, I explain more about why we should not choose to misbehave.

I still wanted a better understanding of God and the world. Why had He allowed me to suffer? Was I being punished for not being good enough?

When I went with a friend to a church group for college students, I realized I was searching for a reason to reconnect with God. I started going to church occasionally and praying whenever I remembered to. I read books about the basics of Christian theology and faith.

At the same time, though, I was busy with school, a part-time job, a boyfriend, and taking care of a dog and a ferret. (Being a Christian is a lot easier when your mom wakes you up every Sunday morning and drops you off at youth group on Wednesday nights.) I still wanted to live my life my way; I just wanted God to be a part of it.

After college graduation, I married, got a full-time job, and moved to a new city. I tried a few churches and found one where I felt welcome. The more I spent time with God and His people, the more I wanted to. I listened to Christian rock on the radio. I volunteered with the youth group and made good friends with some of the other leaders. I joined a ladies' Bible study group and made more friends. Some of us continued meeting together for about ten years.

Some of it must have sunk in, because my life had a focus and meaning I never experienced before. I can look back now and see the evidence of God's work in my life, even when I couldn't see or feel Him. I still don't have all the answers, but that's okay. My role as a Christian isn't to understand all the important things; it's to trust that God does. As I have grown in my faith and obedience, wisdom and peace have grown. Jesus is in me. And I know now that He was there all along.

The next chapter in my story is to share what I have learned with people who are still trying to figure out their stories. Writing a book isn't the only way to do that, but writing has always been a talent of mine. I'm not writing because I have something new to say that you've never heard before. But I've learned a lot from a wide variety of sources throughout my life, and my goal is to put some of the most important ideas together in one place so that someone reading this will have a bit of a leg-up on their journey toward knowing God.

My guess is that most people reading this book will believe in Jesus. But maybe not. What about you? Have you accepted Jesus as the Lord of your life? If not, do you want to? Maybe you've prayed to accept Jesus but you don't see evidence of Him working in your life. You believe in God, but you don't know how to walk with Him.

Do you feel like you must be missing something? Like your life hasn't changed the way you thought it would? Maybe you think you're doing it wrong because other Christians seem so secure and you have more questions than answers.

I was right there for years. I understand what it's like to want to believe but feel like you don't know how. You want to be a good Christian, but you don't want to do the things good Christians do. You desire to do the right thing, but you're not sure that will really happen. You want answers, but the more you ask and seek, the more questions you have.

All your life you've believed what you've been told, and now you want to see it for yourself. But you don't know where to look. Or you've found the answers, and you know they're true, but they aren't what you were hoping for. So you have to decide: Do you follow what's true and what you know is good for you? Or do you hang on to doing things your own way, even when that isn't working out the way you planned?

I also know what it's like when you start making choices based on what you believe is best for you rather than what you want right now. You go to church, read your Bible, pray every day (even though you don't know if you're doing it right), but nothing really changes. You do those things because you know you're supposed to, but you don't enjoy them. You still don't know much about life or God. And you don't see answers to your prayers. You're wondering if it's all worth it.

I have good news for you! If you faithfully continue to seek God and truth, those feelings of uncertainty and dissatisfaction will eventually diminish. As you learn how good God is, you'll discover that even when you don't understand everything about Him, you can trust that He is good. You can see God working in your life and all around you. You can experience joy like you never have before.

If you already know there is a God who is good and you're ready to follow His ways, but you don't know the next step, I know what that's like, too. You want to do more than just be a good person. You want to get the abundant life Jesus said we could have.[2] You'll want to be part of Jesus's team, not just His fan.

Aside from not lying, cheating, stealing, or doing drugs, what can you do for God? How do you know what He wants you to do and what kind of person He wants you to be? Maybe you've heard Christians talk about having a "walk with Jesus," but you don't know what they're talking about. Or you know the faith habits they practice, but you don't get why.

I spent several years figuring out how to get started. Then one day I realized I was already doing it! The searching *is* the doing.

There are two things I've learned are true: There are answers, and God has the answers. Trusting that He knows it all will enable you to experience the kind of life you've been hoping for.

In the rest of this book I'll be adding more detail to those two statements, showing you what they really mean and how they can be true.

---

2   John 10:10.

CHAPTER 2

So how am I gonna get faith?

D o you know a Christian woman who *really* believes in God and the Bible? Someone who prays about everything and believes her prayers will be heard and answered? Someone who does incredible things, like quitting her job to work at a low-paying charity, committing to serve in a foreign country for a year, or adopting a child with special needs? Maybe you've thought, *I wish I was as brave as she is,* or, *If God blessed me the way He has her, I could really serve too.*

It isn't courage or luck that gives some people unusual success, brings answers to their prayers, and fills them with strength and energy to do incredible things. It's faith.

Would you say that you have faith in God? But how much faith do you have? Faith isn't an on/off switch. It's more like a measuring cup that can be filled a little or a lot. And faith isn't so much something you have as something you do.

Let's start with the basics: What does the word *faith* mean? The *Merriam-Webster Dictionary* defines *faith* as "belief and trust in God" or "complete trust."[3] Trust is a necessary component of faith.

The author of the biblical book of Hebrews explains faith as "confidence in what we hope for and assurance about what we do not see" (11:1). He goes on to list many Bible characters who were known for having a lot of faith. He says that Noah, Abraham, and others had faith because they believed the promises God made to them.[4]

In his letter to the Ephesians, Paul, one of the main authors of the New Testament, states that faith, or belief, gives us salvation.[5] We believe that we have been made righteous by Christ's sacrifice, even when we cannot see it and sometimes don't feel like it. Because we believe this promise, it is fulfilled.

However, faith isn't only a matter of knowledge and belief. It's also acting on your beliefs, moving ahead as if something were true even before you have the proof. If you fully believe that God is in control and that His plan for your life is good, you will follow that plan.

Consider this analogy. If you're sick, you go to a doctor, and if he prescribes you some medicine, you take it. You trust he will give you something that will do more good for you than harm. You may not understand how the medicine works, but you believe the doctor knows how to make you feel better and that he intends to do just that. You wouldn't think that merely talking to the doctor, and not taking the medicine, would make you better. You have to take his prescribed course of action.

In the same way, if you trust that God is all-knowing and wants good for your life, you will do what He asks you to do. You believe that when you do, the results will be good for you.

---

3   *The Merriam-Webster Dictionary* (2016), s.v. "faith."
4   Hebrews 11:4–39.
5   Ephesians 1:13–14; 2:8.

You may have heard the saying "Faith without deeds is dead." That comes from the letter written by James, the half-brother of Jesus (James 2:26). He explained his claim using the example of Abraham in the book of Genesis, who was willing to sacrifice his son Isaac because God had promised to give Abraham many descendants through him.[6] James says, "You see that his faith and his actions were working together, and his faith was made complete by what he did" (2:22). A claim to have faith isn't true unless you can prove it by your behavior.

When you act on your faith, you are teaming up with God to work toward His plan. Because God is powerful and faithful, when you work together with Him you will have success and see results.

There are many other examples in the Old and New Testaments of people whose faith worked for them: Noah, Moses, Joshua, and a woman who had been sick for many years. She reached out to touch Jesus's cloak, believing she'd be healed, and she was. Jesus told her, "Your faith has healed you" (Matthew 9:20–22). Her faith was in her action. Her action was motivated by her belief. She got the desired result because she took the action.

Another example of a person in the Bible who showed a lot of faith and saw miraculous results is Gideon.[7] Gideon lived in ancient Israel when it was a young country without a strong military. The people from the neighboring tribes regularly plundered Israel, and God chose Gideon to lead a defense. Gideon had doubts initially; he wasn't a leader or from an important family. But God promised, through an angel, to be with him.

---

6   If you're not familiar with the story of Abraham, read Genesis 12–25. If a story of child sacrifice scares you off, let me give you this spoiler alert: God stops Abraham from going through with it, and Isaac lives to the ripe old age of 180.

7   Judges 6–8.

God told Gideon to take only three hundred men to fight against an army "thick as locusts" with camels as numerous as "the sand on the seashore" (Judges 7:12). Like any normal person, Gideon felt fear while preparing for the battle, but God gave him a sign through another man's dream, and so he believed. In fact, Gideon told his men, "The LORD has given the Midianite camp into your hands," before the battle even began (verse 15). So Gideon led the Israelites to the enemy camp, and they quickly chased out the enemy.

It wasn't Gideon's strength or the strength of the Israelite army that brought victory but the power of God. Most would have bet against the Israelites, but Gideon believed in God's promise to come through for them.

He didn't say, "The Lord *will* give us the Midianite camp," but, "The Lord *has given* the Midianite camp into your hands."[8] This is what the author of Hebrews meant when he wrote, "Faith is … assurance about what we do not see." There were no outward signs that anything had changed in the Midianite camp until Gideon got there and signaled his men, but he believed God was already working it out. As Gideon took action on that belief, even though he was afraid, he got the result through faith.

Faith can be large or small, and small faith can get the same results as strong faith. Jesus said some people (including His own disciples!) "have so little faith" (Matthew 17:20) while others "have great faith" (15:28). He also said a tiny amount of faith, "as small as a mustard seed," is enough

---

8   Judges 7:15, emphasis added.

to move a mountain (17:20). Since faith is the belief in God to fulfill His promises, it's the power of God, not the power of your faith, that does the work.

Because nothing is impossible for God, nothing is impossible for those who have any amount of faith in Him. Yes, you can access *all* of God's power through faith. Paul wrote to the Ephesians, "I pray ... that you may know ... his incomparably great power for us who believe. That power is the same as the mighty strength he exerted when he raised Christ from the dead" (1:18–20).

You may wonder, *How can I put my faith in God when I don't have much to give?* Remember, when you act as though you believe in God's promises for you, even if you aren't totally sure and don't understand, you're acting on faith. That's the secret of the most faithful people. They don't really know how God will come through for them or how the end result will play out, but they go ahead and move forward anyway because they believe it will be good. This is called "stepping out in faith." You take the first step even when you don't know the whole plan and rely on God to make it all work out according to His will. Just like Gideon going into the enemy camp, even though he was afraid.

Let me give you one more example of active faith. At my day job, I'm a middle school teacher. Most people, when they first learn where I work, say I must be really brave. In actuality, I really enjoy teaching young teens. Yeah, they can be rude sometimes, but they can also be pretty funny, and it's great to see these kids turn into "real people."

A couple of years ago, I thought part of God's plan for my life was for my husband and me to move away from where we were living in California and for me to work in a new school. I prayed that God would help me find a teaching job somewhere that I was needed. My husband was offered a job in Oregon, so I started to apply for teaching positions around the same area. Within two weeks, the COVID-19 pandemic hit, and everything went into lockdown. When it was time for me to interview with a couple of schools, the interviews had to be conducted online. I talked to each of the principals on the phone, but I was unable to visit any campuses or meet in person the administrators or teachers I'd be working with.

From the basic impressions I got, one of the schools felt like a good fit for me, the type of school I'd want to work in. But I continued to pray that God would find the right place for me. About a week later, I got a call from the principal of that school offering me a position. However, he said that some funding the school had been expecting was going to be delayed, or possibly lost, due to the pandemic, and he didn't know what specifically I would be teaching or even what grade level.

Accepting the offer would mean selling our house, moving to a new state, finding a place to live, starting work in a new school in a new district, and committing to a one-year contract to teach whatever they needed me to teach ... during a pandemic. Passing on the offer would mean my husband also giving up the job he'd just been offered, staying where we were in the house we already owned, and me keeping the same secure position I was in.

I believed that God would be with me anywhere I lived or worked. But I chose to have faith that God was answering my prayer of a teaching job where I could bless other people. I had no idea how all the details were going to work out—whether I'd still be at the school after a year, if I'd make friends with my colleagues, if my husband and I would buy another house, or how long we would live in Oregon. But since I trust God to know what's best for me, I don't need to know how everything will end up. I just have to take the step He calls me to, believing it will pay off somehow.

In faith, I accepted the position, submitted a resignation to my district, and started packing and getting our house ready to sell. I was acting as if I knew it would all work out, because even though I couldn't see it yet, I believed it.

Once you've learned how to live by faith, you can strengthen and grow your faith. Although small faith will get results, Jesus praises those who have "great faith" (Matthew 8:10) and glorify God in their faithfulness.

We can learn from the examples we've seen and others in the Bible that a person who has strong faith will persevere.

Some wait many years to see the results of their faith. Others work hard without experiencing results, knowing their efforts will eventually be rewarded.

James tells us our faith will be tested, but that's good for us. We become more mature, and our faith grows stronger when it is tested and we persevere.[9]

There's another way we can use and strengthen our faith. Paul called it a "shield ... with which you can extinguish all the flaming arrows of the evil one" (Ephesians 6:16). Some people don't believe in the devil, but the Bible clearly claims that he is real.[10] His number-one aim is to separate you from God. So as you learn to live obediently, wisely, and peacefully, he is going to try to take you down.

His main weapon is deception. His "flaming arrows" are lies, meant to keep you from believing that God's "mighty power" (v. 10) is accessible

---

9   James 1:2–4.
10   John 8:44.

to you. If you ever think, *My faith isn't strong enough* or *Those people are more godly than I am, so I should leave it to them*, you've been deceived by the father of lies.

How can faith shield and protect you from those zingers? Believe in God's Word. He has some very different things to say about you. Jesus said that even if your faith is small, you can still see results. Paul said that God's full strength is available to *all* who believe. If you trust in His promises and step out in faith, even when the little voice in your head says you are acting like a fool and you're bound for failure, you'll see God come through for you. Over time, those lies won't deceive you anymore.

If faith is misplaced, and you start believing in your own strength or righteousness, you will not have the power of God behind your work. Faith isn't believing that God will do whatever you want; it's believing in the promises He made. In another of Paul's letters, he warns us that our faith should "not rest on human wisdom, but on God's power" (1 Corinthians 2:5). This advice is just as relevant today as it was two thousand years ago.

You may have heard preachers say that if you have faith, you will get anything you ask for, like winning the lottery. Or that if you send them money, you are guaranteed to get it back several times over. That sounds like they're asking you to step out in faith. But that's not actually biblical. The verses they use to support their claims are misinterpreted or not taken in the context of the overall message of the Bible.

Jesus does offer us abundant life, but not earthly riches. In fact, He instructed some people to give away everything they owned. It's not how strongly you believe in something, or how much you want it that makes it come true. Rely on the power of God and His promises in Scripture, and you will see the results of your faith.

How can you know God's promises to you? The best way is to read them in the way He gave them to us: the Bible. The book of Proverbs, one of the Bible's books of wisdom, says, "Trust in the LORD with all your heart and lean not on your own understanding; in all your ways submit to him, and he will make your paths straight" (3:5–6). God has promised that if you put your trust in His plan for your life and walk in faith, instead of trying to work everything out by yourself, He will bring His plan to fruition.

One way you can step out in faith on this promise is to pray daily for God's will to be done in your life. It's okay to admit you don't know His plan for you and you're not sure what He wants you to be doing. But ask Him to be in control of your life, to make your path straight, to let His will be done for you and through you. Then be on the lookout for the ways He guides you.

CHAPTER 3

Why would I want to be more obedient?

O bedience is doing what God wants you to do and not doing what He doesn't want you to do. The opposite is sin. Some of it's pretty obvious, such as don't steal or kill or lie. Some of it's harder to decipher, like how often you should go to church. In some areas, God may ask me to do one thing but ask you to do something else. At a certain time in your life, He may ask you to do something, such as take a full-time ministry position, that you weren't ready for previously. I'm not saying there's no such thing as right and wrong. The Bible makes it clear there are certain rules we must all follow. But understanding obedience goes further than knowing a list of rules and being a "good girl" or "good boy."

The issue of obedience can be complicated by the idea of righteousness. We are cleansed of our sins when we believe in Jesus Christ as our Savior. This righteousness is perfect and permanent. If you're not completely obedient all the time, you won't lose your righteousness or your salvation. But anyone who has truly been saved will want to live more obediently.

The concept is similar to the conjunction of faith and action. Just as your actions demonstrate your faith, if you believe that Christ has made you righteous, you will choose to live life His way. If you appreciate the complete purity Jesus covers you with, you will want to be worthy of that gift. Because God is the Lord and Creator of everything, and because He gave you unearned salvation, you will choose to live the way He wants you to. Your obedience is a demonstration of your belief that God's way is the best way.

If you trust God, you will believe that the things He wants you to do will be good for you and those around you and that they will lead to His plan for you being fulfilled. You will also understand that the things He doesn't want you to do would be harmful. Some things will actually cause you physical harm (such as drug use). Other choices will take you off the path toward the blessings God has in store for you.

Knowing the truth will help you understand that sin is bad. Trusting God will help you avoid it. Sin breaks down our relationship with God,[11] which is what our enemy wants to happen.

The devil will tell lies that tempt you to sin. Have you ever had a craving for something, and in that moment you thought you really needed it even though, realistically, you would have survived without it? That's the work of the devil. For example, many times I have thought, *I'm so hungry. I need a snack right now!* I wasn't literally in danger of starving. And eating an extra snack isn't the end of the world. But the more often I make those choices, the more they become habitual, and the further I get from the life God has chosen for me. When I trust God's warnings against gluttony, I choose to make the healthier choice.

---

11   1 John 1:6.

Some people believe in God yet claim there's no such thing as right and wrong. Others comment, usually rhetorically as an argument against Christianity, that since we have been made righteous by Christ's blood, our actions don't matter. Neither of these ideas is supported by the Bible.

The four most important leaders of the early church, Peter, John, James, and Paul, all wrote letters to other believers specifying that there are right and wrong behaviors, and it matters which we choose.

John wrote, "God is light; in him there is no darkness at all. If we claim to have fellowship with him and yet walk in the darkness, we lie and do not live out the truth. But if we walk in the light, as he is in the light, we have fellowship with one another" (1 John 1:5–7). John used light as a metaphor for obedience and darkness for sin. He states that in order to have a good relationship with God and other people, we should obey God, and if we say we're Christians but continue to sin, we are fooling ourselves.

All four of these authors include in their letters lists of specific ways to be obedient. Examples include serving God, being hopeful and patient, and sharing what you have;[12] taking care of widows and orphans;[13] being compassionate and humble;[14] and loving others.[15] They also list sinful behaviors to avoid (such as idolatry and witchcraft;[16] envy and selfishness;[17] malice, deceit, and hypocrisy;[18] and hatred).[19]

Jesus Himself gave commands for His believers to follow, things we must do and things we must not do. All four of Jesus's biographers quote Him teaching about obedience.

∞∞

12　Romans 12:11–13.
13　James 1:27.
14　1 Peter 3:8.
15　1 John 3:23.
16　Galatians 5:20.
17　James 3:14.
18　1 Peter 2:1.
19　1 John 2:11.

Here are some things Jesus said about obedience:

- "Everyone who does evil hates the light, and will not come into the light for fear that their deeds will be exposed. But whoever lives by the truth comes into the light, so that it may be seen plainly that what they have done has been done through God." (John 3:20–21)
- "If your hand causes you to stumble, cut it off. It is better for you to enter life maimed than with two hands to go into hell." (Mark 9:43)
- "Unless you repent, you too will all perish." (Luke 13:3)
- "Anyone who sets aside one of the least of these commands and teaches others accordingly will be called least in the kingdom of heaven, but whoever practices and teaches these commands will be called great in the kingdom of heaven." (Matthew 5:19)

These statements all have a common underlying assumption: that there are right behaviors and wrong behaviors, and Jesus wants His followers to do the right things, because they will lead to a better life.

There have probably been times when you made mistakes and chose something you knew wasn't what God wanted. And there will likely be more of those times in your future. All humans make occasional mistakes. God will not punish you for disobedience, but there may be natural consequences of your actions. If you put your hand on a hot stove, you will get burned. (I'm not saying it's a sin to touch the stove, just a really dumb idea.) Likewise, if you lie to someone, you will likely suffer damage to your relationship and lose trust in the other person's eyes. These types of consequences are the reason God set some behaviors as off-limits.

If you are already suffering the consequences of past sin, the best thing you can do is take it as an opportunity to learn how to better trust and obey God.

Although people use the word *consequence* mostly with negative effects, it refers to whatever events result, both negative and positive. Just as there are consequences of bad decisions, there are consequences from choosing obedience; for example, increased connection with God, greater maturity, more moral strength, and freedom from guilt. If you trust God that the rewards of obedience will be better than whatever gratification you could receive from sin, you will value and choose obedience.

Moses is one example of someone who experienced negative consequences for disobeying God. He led the Israelites after they left slavery in Egypt and traveled to the land God promised would be their home. They had to travel a long way through the desert on foot before they became the nation of Israel. On their journey, the people complained of hunger and thirst.[20]

Twice Moses asked God to provide water for the people, and both times God gave Moses specific directions to follow. The first time, God told Moses to strike a rock with his staff, and when Moses did as he was told, water flowed out.[21]

---

20   Exodus 15:22–24.
21   Exodus 17:6.

A couple of months later, Moses asked God to provide water again. This time, God directed him to tell the rock to let water flow out. Instead of obeying God's specific directions, Moses hit the rock the way he had the first time. Water did flow out, but because Moses was disobedient, God told him he would never set foot in the land promised to the Israelites. And he didn't. The people took possession of their land forty years later, after Moses's death.[22]

We aren't meant to learn about talking to rocks from this example. The lesson is about listening to God. He knows the situations we're in and the plans He has for us. If we trust Him, we will believe that whatever He asks us to do at any moment will be best for us.

Sometimes what He asks changes as we grow or our circumstances change, just as the directions for bringing water out of the rock changed from one instance to the other. We must continue to do what we know is right and listen carefully to God for how He would have us act in each new situation.

Sometimes it's difficult to be obedient to God because we live in such an imperfect world. The first book of the Bible, Genesis, tells the story of how the world was created and how it got messed up.[23]

In the beginning, God made a perfect world, and He made humans to live in it with Him. He gave them free will, but it wouldn't be *truly* free will unless they had a choice to make. Unfortunately, our first ancestors chose the wrong option, desiring to be more like God instead of trusting

---

22   Numbers 20:6–12.
23   Genesis 1–3. If you are new to the Bible, this is another "must read" section.

Him. This bad choice was sin, and sin always leads to pain, sadness, and frustration. Everything that was perfect in the world was tarnished by that action: our planet, the things living on it, relationships with God and other people, even our bodies. That's why we're mortal. It's also why we have sinful desires, also called our *sinful flesh*. We often want things that aren't the best for us and those we care about.

When we accept salvation through Christ, we receive righteousness that restores our relationship with God and guarantees our eternal life. But it does not cure our flesh of temptation. There will always be enticing things that are outside of God's plan for our lives. These temptations vary from person to person. Some people have strong impulses to act violently at times, others feel a need to gather wealth by any means necessary, and some people are tempted to seek physical pleasure through drugs, alcohol, sex, or overeating.

Daniel is an example of someone in the Bible who was obedient to God despite his temptations. He was a prophet from ancient Israel who was taken as a captive to live in Babylon when he was a young man. He and many others were trained to serve the king. At that time, the Israelites followed strict laws about foods they would and would not eat. These laws were given to them by God when they followed Moses out of Egypt. The food laws were meant to keep the people clean, because Jesus had not yet come to cleanse us from all our sins.

The Babylonians did not observe these laws, and the leaders who were feeding the young men gave them the same foods and drinks that were served to the Babylonian royal family. Daniel refused to eat them. He asked instead to be provided with only vegetables and water.[24] The Bible does not specify what kinds of foods the Babylonians were eating. It's possible that some of it was "unclean." Or maybe their cooking and

---

24   Daniel 1:3–12.

serving methods were completely unacceptable to the Israelites. Either way, Daniel decided not to chance it.

Daniel chose obedience when he could easily have gone along with the crowd. The food was already prepared. If it was being served in the Babylonian royal household, it must have been of the highest quality. Most of the group accepted what was given to them. Only Daniel made a different request, and three of his friends followed his lead.

Sometimes it's easy to take the option that's just a little bit bad for us. Most of the young Israelites probably thought:

It would be rude not to take this food they're offering.

If it's good enough for the king, it can't be that bad for me.

I can pick around the worst parts and only eat the foods that are kind of okay.

But Daniel knew the danger of that kind of thinking. When we start to justify bad behaviors, it's easy to lose track of what's right and wrong. First it's *I'll do this but not that.* Then it becomes *I'll only do that a little bit.* Eventually you start thinking, *That hasn't hurt me yet, so I might as well keep doing it.* But the consequences will catch up. Sometimes they pile up early on, but your thinking is so clouded you aren't able to realize what's causing them.

This is one reason being obedient looks different for different people. Temptation is what messes up our thinking. When we're tempted, our emotions and desires outweigh our intelligence. For some people, alcohol is very tempting. And when they drink it, they want it even more. The desire becomes so strong, they feel unable to stop.

I do not have a problem with temptation from alcohol. It's not difficult for me to pass up a drink when I know it's not a wise time to have one. Food, specifically sweets, is my most challenging temptation. If someone offers me a cookie or cupcake, I have a very strong desire to eat it, whether or not I'm hungry.

You might find that food, alcohol, video games, gambling, smoking, the opposite sex, or something completely different causes those temptations for you. You know when something is tempting you if you find yourself regularly agreeing to, taking, or doing something, even when you hadn't planned on it, just because you could.

Smoking and alcohol can be bad for your body, especially if you overdo it, but you might think one cookie isn't going to hurt you. But Jesus said, "No one can serve two masters. Either you will hate the one and love the other, or you will be devoted to the one and despise the other" (Matthew 6:24). He was talking about greed for money, but the same principle applies to temptations of any kind. The more you let something control your life, the harder it will be for you to know what God wants you to do.

That's why we have to follow Daniel's example and not give in even a little bit. You may have to set clear boundaries for yourself in certain areas of your life where you are most tempted. For example, I don't allow myself to eat donuts. I haven't had a donut in five years, because I know that when I see that pink box I will stop thinking clearly and obey my sweet tooth.

As your trust in God grows, you will be better able to resist the temptations of your flesh, but they will not just disappear. Don't get discouraged when you have sinful desires. That doesn't mean you're a bad Christian. Even the most holy people face temptations. But when you trust God, you are able to live obediently despite the temptation.

Though it can be challenging to resist temptation, it is possible for those who trust in God. In 2 Corinthians 10:4–5, Paul wrote, "The weapons we fight with ... have divine power to demolish strongholds. We demolish arguments and every pretension that sets itself up against the knowledge of God, and we take captive every thought to make it obedient to Christ." Faith is one of our weapons. And faith does not operate on human power but on God's divine power.

Another of our weapons is knowledge of what's good and bad for us. We can use that knowledge to demolish the lies we might use to justify bad behavior.

John explained it this way: "[God's] commands are not burdensome, for everyone born of God overcomes the world. This is the victory that has overcome the world, even our faith" (1 John 5:3–4). It's easier to obey God's commands if you trust that He is more powerful than the forces of this world and that when you are living life His way, that power works for your good.

If you feel tempted to try something you know could be dangerous, remind yourself that God does not want you to come to harm. Trust that He wants you to avoid those behaviors because of His love for you. And remember that the Holy Spirit has given you strength to do His will ... the same strength God used when He brought Jesus back to life!

Paul wrote about "fruit of the Spirit," which includes "goodness, faithfulness ... and self-control" (Galatians 5:22–23). Those who are faithful, good, and in control of themselves will have the result of a highly obedient life.

These fruits, or benefits, are "of the Spirit," not of a Christian or of a good person. Paul isn't saying we should just decide to have self-control. In order to have those qualities in our lives, we need to rely on the Spirit to work in us and make us more like God so we are able to obey.

Jesus also used the metaphor of fruit. He said, "No branch can bear fruit by itself; it must remain in the vine. Neither can you bear fruit unless you remain in me" (John 15:4). Once we know what fruit He is offering, we can see that we will never be perfectly good on our own, no matter how hard we try. The best way for us to live more obediently is to live "in Him."

Jesus repeatedly commanded His followers to love people.[25] Sounds nice, doesn't it? If we all obeyed that command, what a wonderful world it would be.

Jesus told us to love not just our friends but even our enemies.[26] Now, that seems a lot harder. It's definitely a test of obedience.

Another of His commands is to not judge others.[27] Jesus was clear that it's not our responsibility to decide who is and isn't doing a good job of being obedient. Whether it's that person you can't stand or someone you love who is momentarily getting on your nerves, the times when it's hard to love someone are when we most need to trust God.

Not judging truly requires trusting God. Believing that God is in control when others are doing things we don't think they should and trusting Him to take care of people we think are making mistakes is the only way to avoid judging them. We have to have faith that God will judge the righteous and the unrighteous.

Becoming perfect and complete is a long and trying process that will not be finished in this lifetime. Even many Christian leaders struggle with anger, pride, greed, and other sins. We must give grace to others as well as to ourselves.

Until we accept God's gift of the Holy Spirit, we do not have the power of Christ to overcome temptation. That's why Christ came for us while we

---

25   Matthew 22:39.
26   Matthew 5:44.
27   Matthew 7:1.

were still in our sin. He didn't wait for us to live perfectly before offering salvation, because no one would ever be worthy of salvation. Therefore, we can't expect unbelievers to become righteous on their own. If you see someone who's not a Christian sinning, don't judge them. They may not understand why their decisions are sinful, and if they do, they probably don't know how to overcome the temptation. The best thing you can do for that person isn't to point out what they're doing wrong. Help them come to know Jesus, and live your life in a way that would make them want to.

No one but Jesus is perfect. You've made mistakes and sometimes chosen disobedience, and God has been merciful and forgiven you. It would be a sin of pride to think you ought to judge another person.

As you've been reading this chapter, have you been thinking about behaviors or activities that you've heard Christians label as sins? Have you felt uncomfortable because you think you may have participated in some of them? Or are you regularly participating in one or more sins? The first thing I want you to know is you're not alone. All people occasionally sin; no one is perfect. That's why Jesus had to die on the cross for all of us.

The other thing you should know is that if you have accepted Jesus as your Savior and received the gift of the Holy Spirit, you will feel convicted when you make wrong choices. God speaks to you through the Holy Spirit to tell you what's right and wrong and help you become more obedient.

Maybe you've been feeling frustrated because you want to be a better person. Or you're a pretty good person, but there's one thing you do that you wish you wouldn't. Maybe it's not even something bad, just something you don't want to do because that's not the kind of person you want to be. Perhaps you get really angry at annoying people. Or you feel jealous when a friend gets something you want or does something cool. Or you argue with your family a lot, and even though you know you're right most of the time, you still think it would be better to try to get along.

If you're feeling conviction over choices you've made or bad attitudes or actions that have become habits, you don't need to be ashamed or defeated. You are forgiven for all past sins, and you have the power of Christ to resist the temptation to make those same mistakes again.

Now that you have a better understanding of why it's best for you to live in accordance with God's desires for your life, you can trust Him as you work at being more obedient. If you know there's something you should stop doing, don't just try harder to stop doing it. Put your trust in God and engage with Him more.

People talk about needing willpower to accomplish something great. But willpower is only the beginning. Your willpower is your decision to obey God. But the lies of the devil and the temptations of your flesh can be stronger than your will. That's when you need to depend on the power of Christ in you.

If you try to have more self-control through willpower alone, you won't see much change. Humans have a limited amount of willpower. If you attempt to quit a bad habit cold turkey, without changing anything else, you will probably only succeed for a limited time and then give in. To stop doing something you think God doesn't want you to do anymore, think about what you will do more of.

I'm not encouraging you to keep doing what you know you shouldn't be doing or to do whatever you want without limits or control, especially if you're involved in any dangerous behaviors. Choose to do what's right. Choose to do better. Try not to mess up in the same way again. But if you do, don't give up and think you aren't strong enough. We have all of God's strength available to us. Don't beat yourself up or entertain bad thoughts about yourself. Think about what happened and why. What situation were you in when you made that wrong choice? What could you do differently next time? How might you avoid similar situations?

Instead of spending a lot of time thinking about what you shouldn't do, learn more about God and why He is trustworthy. Consider how He wants you to work for Him in faith, and practice trusting Him with that.

Obedience isn't always the natural state of behavior, at least for me. To continue to be obedient, I have to be conscious of my actions and choose the ones that align with God's will. I don't think of myself as a depraved, evil person, but I certainly have some bad habits.

Two of the hardest attitudes for me to overcome are selfishness and laziness. I'm not often tempted to sin in ways that would actively harm others, but I don't always want to do what I know God wants me to do, because it's simply easier not to. But I will miss out on many of the blessings He wants me to bring into the world if I don't act on His plan for me.

One way I've had to specifically choose to be obedient is in writing and publishing this book. I enjoy writing. I've written a lot of things in my life: poems, short stories, a blog, a master's thesis. I may not be the next Hemingway, but I feel pretty adept at writing. I have always known it was a talent gifted to me by God to be used for His glory.

But until I was in my mid-thirties, I never attempted to write *about* God. Writing requires not only talent, but also content. For a long time I didn't feel I knew enough about God to write anything worth anyone's time. But I have spent over thirty years learning about God and how to live His way, from other authors and from real-life lessons.

I recently attended a Christian women's conference, and as I was listening to one of my favorite authors speak, I felt God translating her message for me in my heart, and I knew He was saying, "It's time for you to write and share what you've learned."

It's exciting to be working on something that I know God will use for His purposes. Even if very few people ever read this book, and the only one who learns anything from it is myself, it's God's will, and I get to see it being produced. I trust that if He has asked me to do this, He has a plan to use it, and I don't need to know the whole plan right now.

But sometimes I don't feel like writing. I don't dislike doing it. I'm just not in the mood. For me, starting to write takes a lot of energy and focus. Once I get going, I can pour out words for hours, but getting started each day is always the hard part.

To be honest, there have been many days when I've made the wrong choice. I had time to write but chose to do something less important, like watch TV. Other days, even though it felt nearly impossible to drag myself off the couch and get to work, I chose to do it by reminding myself that I can trust God to help me because He asked me to do this work with Him.

I've also dealt with some fear and trepidation as I got closer to finishing writing the manuscript because I don't have any experience with the publishing process. The more I learn about it, the more I realize how difficult it is. My skills are in writing, not negotiation, promotion, marketing, or design. I'm going to have to face those fears, reach out for help, and trust God to make things happen that are out of my control. So if this book has been published and you're reading it, that means I chose obedience enough times to get it done.

Being obedient to God means following the plan He has for you. Part of that obedience is not doing things that will distract you from His plan. If you're like me, you can find any number of distractions: watching television, reading books, browsing the internet, playing video games, scrolling through social media. None of these things are necessarily evil or sinful. In fact, they can be used for good. But we need to take a look at our lives every once in a while to make sure nothing is getting in the way of the things God is asking us to do. If you notice that you spend more time during your day being entertained than working to make the world more like God's kingdom, think seriously about how that can be changed.

You may become distracted from true obedience by comparing yourself to others. You see Christians doing things that seem good and important—and they probably are, for *them*. That doesn't mean you need to be doing the same things. For example, you might have a friend who's super involved in church activities. Maybe she volunteers to pass out bulletins at weekly services and helps set up for special events. That ministry of service is a wonderful way for her to bless others, if that's what God is leading her to do now. That does not mean you should feel guilty or overwork yourself trying to keep up if God has different plans for your time. He might want you to study theology, raise a family, serve your community through a nonprofit organization, or write a book.

Because we are all unique individuals with different characteristics, talents, and passions, God uses each of us in different ways. Paul compared us to the parts of a body. In his letter to Jesus's followers in the city of Corinth, he wrote:

> The body is not made up of one part but of many. ... If the whole body were an eye, where would the sense of hearing be? If the whole body were an ear, where would the sense of smell be? But in fact God has placed the parts in the body, every one of them, just as he wanted them to be. (1 Corinthians 12:14, 17–18)

Don't confuse doing more with being obedient. And don't let yourself be distracted by what other people are doing. Ask God to show you His plan for you.

In order to live obediently, you need to know what God says is right and wrong and what His plan for you is. There are some commands Jesus told us all to follow. You and I are required to love God and other people,[28] be generous and give to those in need,[29] and be honest and keep our promises.[30] However, in other ways, obedience can be different for different people, and your situation in life may dictate how you can live for God. For example married people and single people should not live the same way.

Reading the Bible and praying will help you live in obedience, as well as faith. From the Bible's many stories of obedient and disobedient people, you can get an idea of the types of things God wants His people to do and in what situations He gives people particular commands. Some might not apply directly to your life. For example, God is probably not asking you to lead an army, like Gideon, but you can pick up some patterns from his story and see how they apply to the circumstances you find yourself in.

Praying—speaking to God and listening to Him—is another effective action to build a more obedient life. Listen for God's direction before you make an important decision. Your conscience will remind you of what you already know you should do.

---

28   Matthew 22:37–39.
29   Matthew 5:42.
30   Matthew 5:37.

What if you know what you should do but you don't want to do it? Tell God you trust that His commands are for your own good and ask Him to make it easier for you to be obedient. Follow the example of the psalmist who wrote, "Turn my heart toward your statutes and not toward selfish gain. Turn my eyes away from worthless things; preserve my life according to your word" (Psalm 119:36–37). You can ask God to remove the temptation, but then you have to do what you know is right.

Spend time in fellowship with other Christians who have more experience and can tell you when you seem to be heading the wrong way. Some of our sins are obvious to us, but in other ways we can be good at misleading ourselves. Temptation can trick us into making excuses or telling ourselves that if others do it, it must be okay. That's why we need trustworthy people in our lives. Surround yourself with the type of people who seem good at living in tune with God's will, and ask them if they see anything in your life you should or should not be doing. Then ask them to pray for you as you seek God's direction in those areas.

CHAPTER 4

Can I really get wiser?

Do you think you have to be old before you can be wise? Do you assume that before you can start to grow in wisdom, you have to get rid of a ton of foolishness?

We don't have to wait to become wise. If we trust God, our wisdom will grow. And the sooner we start acting with wisdom, the more benefits we will see throughout our lives.

Do you know what wisdom is? It's not the same thing as intelligence. There's some relation between the two, but your wisdom is not limited by your intelligence. Basically, intelligence is how smart you are and how much stuff you've learned. Wisdom is about deciding what to do and when.

For example, intelligence might be knowing how to balance your checkbook. Wisdom is knowing when you should give money to a friend in need.

Wisdom works by giving you a better understanding of who you are and who God is so you can make decisions that fit within that reality.

Suppose a swimmer goes to the beach while a powerful tide is moving out. She believes she's strong enough to swim safely in that fast-moving water, but the current is actually stronger than she is. Swimming out into deep water would be a foolish decision for her. If she had a solid understanding of her own limits and the situation at hand, she would make a wiser choice.

Those who have accepted salvation from Jesus Christ are children of God; that's our identity.[31] To truly understand who we are, we need to understand who our heavenly Father is and what our relationship to Him is. Wise people know that God is the holiest, most powerful, and highest authority. Knowing God and understanding ourselves leads to humility.[32] We understand that trying to take on the authority of God in our own lives is foolish. As Paul put it, "Do not think of yourself more highly than you ought, but rather think of yourself with sober judgment" (Romans 12:3). "Sober judgment," or clear-headed wisdom, will keep us from considering ourselves greater than we really are. The greatest wisdom comes from trusting in God to give us holiness and power and to be our authority.

Wisdom lets us know what's right and wrong and gives us a better idea of God's plan for our lives. We don't see it all at once; God is more mysterious than even the wisest humans can comprehend. But He will give us guidance.

In my life, God often reveals parts of His plan at just the right moment for me to act. Sometimes wisdom is knowing when to be patient.

Paul said we should renew our minds, and that will help us figure out God's will or plan.[33] Keep seeking wisdom to make your thinking and understanding more clear so you will be better able to see your role in God's kingdom.

---

31   1 John 3:1.
32   James 3:13.
33   Romans 12:2.

Wisdom will help you have greater faith and obedience. Faith is an action; we should "step out in faith." But sometimes it's hard to know which direction to step. You may fully believe God can use your deeds for His plan, but you're not certain what His plan is. Wisdom helps you see which direction will lead toward the good things God has for you. Aside from avoiding obvious sins, when you are not sure what God wants you to be doing, wisdom can make obedience clearer.

The most complete and perfect wisdom is simply trusting God. In everything, trust God. With problems, questions, hopes, dreams, struggles, decisions, and habits. With money, health, family, friends, romance, school, employment, and your future.

If you believe that God is all-knowing and all-powerful, and He has a plan for you, the wisest decision you can make is to trust His plan. Choosing to trust Him will be the right decision every time.

Solomon was the third king of ancient Israel, a descendant of Abraham. He is considered by many to be the wisest man who ever lived. We can learn from the wise things he did and also how he sought to be wiser.

After his father, David, died and he became king, Solomon had a dream in which God told him to ask for anything he wanted. Solomon asked for discernment to be able to tell right from wrong, because he wanted to be a good king.[34]

The Lord was pleased that Solomon asked for this. So God said to him:

---

34   1 Kings 3:9.

Since you have asked for this and not for long life or wealth for yourself, nor have asked for the death of your enemies but for discernment in administering justice, I will do what you have asked. I will give you a wise and discerning heart, so that there will never have been anyone like you, nor will there ever be. Moreover, I will give you what you have not asked for—both riches and honor—so that in your lifetime you will have no equal among kings. (1 Kings 3:10–13)

Solomon knew that wisdom, also called judgment or discernment, would help him to be a better king and to better serve God.

God answered Solomon's request for a couple of reasons. He knows it's good for people to have wisdom, especially those in a position of influence. He also appreciated Solomon's pure motives in asking for wisdom in order to help others. Therefore, God also rewarded him with wealth and honor.

Shortly after that dream, Solomon had to settle a difficult court case. He used an understanding of people's hearts and thought outside the box to find out the truth of the matter when there was no physical evidence available.[35] He searched out the truth instead of giving an easy answer. This demonstrated that he had indeed become very wise. Solomon became one of the richest kings to ever live, and he built a temple to God in Jerusalem more magnificent than anything in the world in those days.

God wants us to have wisdom. It will help us do what we set out to do and be what we want to be. Even if we do not want to be a king or queen, wisdom will make us more successful as students, employees, humanitarians, entrepreneurs, or any other area of our lives.

---

35   1 Kings 3:16–27.

A good life and a good reputation will come from getting wisdom. You probably won't become the richest person in the world, but if you are wise, you will know how to make sensible financial and personal decisions, and how people and the world really work, which will benefit you throughout your life.

Gaining wisdom by trusting God is like climbing a ladder. The more you trust God, the wiser you will become, and as your wisdom grows, your trust in God will grow. When you put your foot on the first rung of a ladder and push yourself up, your other foot is closer to the next rung. As you take each step, the next rung becomes easier to reach.

Wisdom comes from knowing that God is in control and you're not. If you trust that His way is the right way, you'll know the best way to handle a situation. Some situations are complicated, and it's not always immediately clear what God's way of handling it would be. That's when you need to seek more wisdom to better understand who God is. As you get to know Him, you'll find out He really is good and faithful. Wisdom both requires trust and builds trust.

I'm no Solomon, but I have grown much wiser than I was earlier in life. I made many foolish mistakes before I began to fervently seek wisdom.

Ten years ago, when my black lab, Ronin, was a year old, he started jumping over our fence to get into the neighbors' yards and wander around the neighborhood. A couple of times he ate things he found and came home sick. We had to take him to the emergency veterinary office more than once.

I felt desperate to rush to a solution. I searched online and found something called a "coyote roller." Usually they're used on the outside of fences to keep coyotes from climbing into a yard, but I figured we could put some on the inside to keep Ronin from getting out.

Having them installed professionally would've cost hundreds of dollars. After looking at a few pictures online, I thought I had a good enough understanding that I could install coyote rollers on our fence with some help from my husband.

We went to Home Depot for screws, brackets, wire, and thick PVC pipes. As we tried to get all that home in my husband's car, I cracked the windshield. That should have given me some humility. But I was so intent on finishing my project that I gave no thought to the wise way to proceed.

While we were trying to assemble all of our pieces on the fence, my husband and I got into an argument about the proper way to proceed. Again, I let fear cloud my judgment. I could not concede that I didn't have the best understanding of the situation. Looking back I cringe at my foolishness. I know that in any kind of mechanical or engineering situation, my level of understanding will always lag behind his.

We finally finished the project. Or at least we reached a point where we didn't think we could improve it any. Although our coyote rollers somewhat resembled the pictures I'd seen, they didn't quite work. Our rollers didn't roll. They didn't stop Ronin from hopping over the fence.

To make matters worse, having all that weight on one side of the fence caused it to tilt. Over time the fence and the rollers leaned in so close to the house we almost couldn't walk through our yard. We ended up replacing the whole fence after a few years.

If I'd been wiser, I would not have let worry drive me to rush into things. I would have sought advice from someone who knew more about fences than I did. I would have humbled myself enough to admit that I did not have the knowledge or skills to take on that project.

If I had put my trust fully in God, I wouldn't have let fear drive my decision-making, my behavior, or my words. Now that I am older and wiser, I trust that God is always with me and for me. I rely on Him to lead me to the best decision in any situation, rather than thinking I need to figure everything out on my own.

To gain wisdom for yourself, run new thoughts about God and ideas for your life by godly people and compare them to what Scripture says. If you are still early into your walk with Jesus, don't be afraid of other people telling you that you're wrong. That's the best way to learn! When you notice patterns in the responses you get from those further along in their Christian journeys, you will make that wisdom your own.

Pray to God for wisdom, like Solomon did. He wants you to have it. He promises to grant it to anyone who seeks it. James wrote, "If any of you lacks wisdom, you should ask God, who gives generously to all without finding fault, and it will be given to you" (1:5). Tell God you understand that wisdom means trusting Him, and you know He wants His people to be wise and to value having wisdom. Ask Him to give you more wisdom and thank Him for promising to give it to anyone who asks.

CHAPTER 5

More peace?
Yes, please!

I want you to close your eyes, sit still, and listen to your thoughts for a few moments. Go ahead, do it now. I'll wait.

What kind of thoughts went through your mind just now? Did you have a happy daydream about cute animals frolicking in the wild? Did you think about how wonderful your family or friends are and how thankful you are to have them? Did you think about all the things you need to get done in the next couple of days? Did you wonder if you were doing it right or how much longer you were supposed to keep your eyes closed?

If your undirected thoughts immediately turn toward an unending flow of questions and worries, or if sitting still for a few minutes gives you anxiety about all the things you could or should be doing, you might benefit from having more peace in your life.

Peace is a sense that things will be okay and an absence of worry or fear. It does not mean you don't wonder about the future or try to do your best. It means you realize that you can't control the future and everyone makes mistakes at times, but you don't let those realities affect your emotional state.

People can reduce their anxiety and increase their peace through meditation and positive self talk, but it's impossible to stay peaceful all the time without God. Tough stuff happens in life, and if you don't have someone bigger than yourself to trust in, you won't always be free from fear.

If you trust God, even when things are not going your way, you won't have to worry, because you know God will take care of all that for you. Proverbs 3:5–6 tells us, "Trust in the Lord. ... In all your ways submit to him, and he will make your paths straight." Notice it doesn't say God will put you on the path that you choose or make your path lead where you want to go. He will bring things into your life and point you toward what He has planned for you.

Knowing that God, who sees all things and knows all things, is choosing for you will bring you peace.[36] It alleviates the stress you might otherwise experience when your path starts going a direction you did not expect. If you can say to yourself, "I have put my trust in God and acknowledge Him as the leader of my life," you will have peace, knowing He is bringing you through life's surprises. If you trust God in everything, you will be at peace. If you believe He can do what He has promised, including working out all things for your good, you will have freedom from worry.

If you fully trust God, you will not worry about bad things happening because you know He is with you, watching over you and working

36   Psalm 147:5.

everything out to your benefit. Even if something you don't want to happen does, you know it's just a piece of His greater plan. That's not to say He caused it to happen, but He allowed it to happen because He knows He can use it to further His plan to do what's good for you.

God wants to give you peace. It's true! He is your loving Father. He doesn't only care about your obedience and your faith. He also cares about your well-being. He has empathy for His children. He feels bad when we feel bad.

One of the most common phrases throughout the Bible is "Do not be afraid." It's used about seventy times by God the Father, Jesus, and angels. Jesus actually commanded us not to worry and followed that up by reminding us we have nothing to worry about because God will take care of us.[37]

Paul wrote to his friends, "May the God of hope fill you with all joy and peace as you trust in him" (Romans 15:13). The peace and joy He has in store for you can only come when you trust Him. If you are turning away from Him and trying to figure everything out on your own, you will miss out on the peace He is offering freely.

Being a middle school teacher is the only job I dreamed of as a kid, and I'm thankful that God fulfilled that for me. However, one experience

---

37   Matthew 6:25–26, 32.

on my job produced major anxiety in me, and I had to lean fully on my trust in God to be at peace.

After much consideration and prayer, I decided to take a group of students on an educational trip to Washington, DC. Preparing for it was a lot of work, but I knew most of my students would not have another opportunity like this, so I felt it would all be worthwhile.

Unfortunately, I am afraid of flying. I know the odds of crashing are less than being struck by lightning, but I still feel afraid every time I'm on a plane. I get nervous long before I get to the airport. And in flight, at every bump and turn, I'm pretty sure we're going down. Furthermore, I really don't like being in confined spaces with a lot of people. I am not claustrophobic, but I am a bit germophobic.

However, the only practical way to get from California to DC is by air. As the date of our trip approached, I had mini panic attacks every time I thought of it. After all, I was responsible for the care and protection of eight children. I had to make sure we all made it to the airport on time in our rented minivan with all our tickets, luggage, food money, etc.

For most of the students, it was their first time in an airplane. My being afraid would not be helpful, so I did my best to assure them and model peace.

I had to decide whether to focus on my fears or to trust that God works out everything according to His will[38] and for the good of His people.[39] I did not know what His will was for us. Of course, I hoped it would be a smooth flight, arriving on time. But that was outside my control. My worry would not have any effect on the outcome. So instead of thinking about everything that could go wrong, I prayed that God would bring me peace, and I trusted that He would be in control.

---

38   Ephesians 1:11.
39   Romans 8:28.

The flight was only a little bumpy. The flight back was all right too. Every time I began to feel nervous, I reminded myself that the Bible says we can have peace, prayed that God would take care of us, and chose again to put my trust in Him. I refused to let anxiety or fear hold me back from everything I needed to do.

If I hadn't been able to put my trust in God, I would not have enjoyed the experience as much as I did.

To have peace in your life, you must be a peacemaker. Sometimes that means apologizing for something you've done wrong and working to make it right. It's hard to feel peace when you have a guilty conscience. And you can't feel peace if you're letting someone else's actions cause you to feel irritated and bitter. So follow Jesus's command to forgive others.[40]

Forgiveness isn't about approving of people's bad behavior or allowing them to do it again. It's about your heart. Forgiveness is letting go of the nasty feelings that another person caused and choosing peace. It isn't wanting to see someone punished. It's truly wishing that person well from your heart.

You may think, *That person does not deserve my forgiveness.* Of course they don't! By definition, forgiveness can't be earned or deserved.

But it isn't easy. Some people who suffer terrible losses have to choose to forgive every day. The temptation to hold on to anger might last a lifetime. But forgiving will benefit you much more than it benefits the other person. It's the only way you'll ever really feel peace.

When Solomon's father, David (the same David who killed the giant Goliath), was young, a man named Saul was king. When King Saul found

---

40   Luke 17:3.

out God had chosen David to replace him, he was furious. He spent twenty years chasing David all around the country and coming up with plots to kill him. David could easily have become angry and bitter and sought revenge. If he hadn't put his trust in God, David may have tried to take control of the situation. He had multiple opportunities to kill Saul, but he let them all pass by. David forgave Saul for his behavior and honored him as king. He attempted, as much as he was able, to create peace between himself and his enemy. And he wept with true grief at Saul's death.[41] He became known as a man after God's own heart.[42]

If you're finding it difficult to trust God enough to stop worrying, or if you trust God but still do not feel peace, here are some actions you can take.

First, pray. When you can't stop thinking about your problems or all the things that could go wrong, ask God to give you peace. Tell Him you know that the way to experience the deepest peace is by trusting Him, and ask Him to help you trust Him and His plan for your life.

Beyond the natural release from worry, if you put your trust in God by praying to Him, He will give you supernatural peace. Paul's letter to the Philippians tells us to "not be anxious about anything, but in every situation, by prayer and petition, with thanksgiving, present your requests to God. And the peace of God, *which transcends all understanding*, will guard your hearts and your minds in Christ Jesus" (4:6–7, emphasis added).

---

41   1 Samuel 16–2 Samuel 1.
42   Acts 13:22.

Paul certainly knew that there are many things in this life we could be anxious about.

His original name was Saul (totally different from the Saul we just talked about). He was a pious Jew who thought he was honoring God by arresting Christians in an attempt to destroy the early church. Then one day, as he was on his way to look for more Christians to imprison, a light from heaven shined so bright that he fell down. He heard the voice of Jesus asking why Saul was persecuting Him. After that, Saul was blind. He refused to eat anything for three days.

God sent a believer named Ananias to talk to Saul and give him miraculous healing. After that, Saul stayed with some Christians, and he confessed his belief in Jesus. He started going by the name Paul. He traveled around the world preaching about forgiveness of sins through Jesus. Many people came to faith by his teachings, and several followed his example to travel and spread the good news.[43]

But Paul's travels did not always go as planned, and he often found himself in unsafe situations. In one of his letters, he said:

> I have been constantly on the move. I have been in danger from rivers, in danger from bandits, in danger from my fellow Jews, in danger from Gentiles; in danger in the city, in danger in the country, in danger at sea; and in danger from false believers. I have labored and toiled and have often gone without sleep; I have known hunger and thirst and have often gone without food; I have been cold and naked. Besides everything else, I face daily the pressure of my concern for all the churches. (2 Corinthians 11:26–28)

---

43   Acts 8–9, 13–28.

And that was *before* he survived a shipwreck.[44]

After going through all that, how could Paul tell anyone to "be anxious for nothing"?

In the same letter as his long list of perils, he said:

> Praise be to the God and Father of our Lord Jesus Christ, the Father of compassion and the God of all comfort, who comforts us in all our troubles, so that we can comfort those in any trouble with the comfort we ourselves receive from God. For just as we share abundantly in the sufferings of Christ, so also our comfort abounds through Christ. ...
>
> We do not want you to be uninformed, brothers and sisters, about the troubles we experienced in the province of Asia. We were under great pressure, far beyond our ability to endure, so that we despaired of life itself. Indeed, we felt we had received the sentence of death. But this happened that we might not rely on ourselves but on God, who raises the dead. (2 Corinthians 1:3–5, 8–9)

I don't know what dangers, labors, toils, hardships and pressures you're dealing with. But if Paul could rely on God when he was facing certain death, you can trust Him in whatever you are going through.

The peace that transcends (goes beyond) understanding doesn't just come from you recognizing that if God is for you there's no reason to fear or worry. It works beyond your own power, regardless of your natural mental or emotional state, to bring an unexplainable sense that you will be okay.

---

44   Acts 27:41.

When you ask God to take care of you and work things out for you, and you decide to trust Him rather than worry, tension will leave your body, like sinking into a tub of warm water. Immerse yourself in the soothing and healing knowledge of His presence.

To experience more peace, memorize Bible verses. Start by copying the three verses previously quoted in this chapter onto a sticky note or index card, including the reference (the name of the book, chapter number, and verse numbers). Read each one and repeat it to yourself several times. Then flip your note over and try to recite it without looking. It's okay if you have to peek now and then until you can say the whole verse without looking.

Reciting your memory verses to yourself once or twice a day is a good way to keep a peaceful mindset. As they become rooted in your mind, you will eventually notice that you think of them when you need them. When you begin to feel fear or anxiety, a verse will come into your mind that reminds you to trust God. That's the work of the Holy Spirit in you.

You can also make a gratitude list.

A gratitude list is a list you make and build over time of different things you're grateful for. When times are hard, or when you're afraid, think of blessings you're thankful for.

If you're not sure where to start, just be grateful you are alive today. Look around you, and you'll find more to appreciate—some important things, some less significant, are improving your life. Don't leave out the little things. Like chocolate. Or cute shoes. You'll probably be able to create a longer list than you first expected.

Definitely include the people you are thankful for, those who are currently in your life or those who influenced you in the past. Family members, friends, teachers, coaches, pastors. A neighbor who helped you out. A custodian who keeps your school or workplace clean. The barista who made your drink exactly the way you like it.

You may think you don't have a lot to be thankful for because your life isn't the way you'd like, or you are lacking one thing you really want. Start a gratitude list anyway. You might surprise yourself with how many good things you can find when you start looking for them. It's natural to focus on our problems or the things we don't have. But thinking about the negatives doesn't bring peace. It can actually wire your brain into negative patterns, even if you get what you've been hoping for!

Making a gratitude list can wire your brain to focus on the positives. That's why Paul wrote, "Do not be anxious about anything" (Philippians 4:6).

Once you've started your list, add to it daily. Challenge yourself to find one new thing you're thankful for each day.

Don't just write it down. Pray your list every day. Start your quiet time by thanking God out loud for the good things in your life that day.

This isn't a menu of options for you to choose from. You will experience peace sooner and more often if you do all three. You will also notice that they work together, like the middle of a Venn diagram, where multiple circles overlap, and you're going back and forth, in and out, combining different practices into one routine.

If you've been doing all these strategies for a while and still rarely feel at peace, you may need to find some professional help. Mental health conditions can get in the way of a peaceful life. If you have any suspicion that you might be experiencing mental health issues, get help to diagnose and treat it right away. Then you can continue with the steps described here.

CHAPTER 6

All that sounds good, but how do I know I can trust God?

I t's not enough for me to say you should trust God, that trusting Him is good for you. You need to know He is worthy of your trust. Even if you think you should, or you want to, if you do not feel able to trust God, you will try, then begin to doubt and get frustrated. So let me give you several reasons why you can trust Him.

We can trust God because He is love. Even before creation, God lived in community as the Trinity. Then He created humans to share His love with. Before Adam and Eve sinned, they had a close relationship with God. He wants to have that kind of relationship with you. That's why He sacrificed His Son, Jesus—to reconnect with us.[45] Loving someone means you want what's best for them, and you're willing to put yourself and your

45   Ephesians 2:16.

own needs second. God gave us a great example of how to love. Because He loves us, we can trust that He wants what's best for us.

We can also trust God because He is faithful. He never changes His mind. He does not have bad days or get tired. He does not give up. He fulfills all His promises. He fulfilled His promise to Abraham that He would bless the world through his son Isaac (an ancestor of Jesus). He was faithful to the Israelites leaving Egypt by staying with them and leading them by a column of smoke and a pillar of fire during the forty years it took them to reach their promised land.[46] The God you read about in the Bible is the same God who is with you today. He is *always* with you. He is *always* for you. He *always* works for your good.

We can trust God because He is holy. Set apart. High above everything and everyone else.[47] No one can be compared to Him. Anything in this world can disappoint you. People may hurt you or let you down. But God isn't swayed by the same influences as people, and He isn't subject to the same limitations as His creation. God alone is able to stand the test of time because He is holy.

We can trust God because He is righteous. God created everything, including the physical laws of nature.[48] He also set the moral laws of the universe. God determined what's good and bad. You can trust Him because He is unfailingly good. Everything He does is right and righteous.

We can trust God because He is all-knowing. He sees the whole picture, from beginning to end, in complete detail.[49] God's wisdom is greater than that of any human. He knows what could happen, what consequences would result from any decision or action. He alone can see what really is best for you.

---

46   Exodus 40:36–38.
47   Deuteronomy 4:39.
48   Genesis 1:3–7.
49   Ecclesiastes 3:11.

We can trust God because He is generous. Jesus stated in His Sermon on the Mount that God gives good gifts to His people.[50] Jesus Himself was a gift from God to the world. Paul wrote that since God is so generous as to give His Son to leave heaven and live on earth to suffer and die, He will certainly be generous enough to give us everything else we need.[51] Why would God pay the price of sacrificing His own Son to cover our sins so we could be brought back into relationship with Him and have eternal life, if He wasn't also willing to meet the needs that would help us remain in that relationship? We can trust God to be generous with us because He doesn't need anything, and He will never run out of strength, energy, power, riches, or resources to give.

We can trust God because He is sovereign. He is the King, the Boss, the Head Honcho, the Lord of all creation. Heaven is His throne, and the earth is His footstool.[52] No one tells Him what to do. He cannot be controlled or manipulated. He always does what He wants, and what He wants is always best for us. He will not let us down.

I hope by now you've decided to put your trust in God. But does your life show it? Or do faith, obedience, wisdom, and peace still seem hard? If so, your decision to trust has not translated into everyday action yet. But don't worry. I have some ideas for how to change that.

I bet you can guess what I'm going tell you to do first. Pray! If you want something from God, ask for it.

Another way you can deepen your trust in God is to get to know Him better.

---

50 Matthew 6:33; 7:11.
51 Romans 8:32.
52 Matthew 34–35.

Imagine you recently met a new friend, and she seems pretty cool. You get along well and have spent a little time having fun and laughing. If you needed someone to feed your cat while you were away from home for two weeks, would you ask this new friend? Probably not. More likely you'd ask someone you've known for a long time, someone who's been helpful in the past, someone who has kept her promises to you.

Building trust takes time. And so does giving the other person opportunities to earn your trust. If this new friend asked to borrow a couple of dollars and promised to pay you back the next day, you might do it. If she didn't pay you back, you'd only be out a couple of bucks, but you'd know more about where your relationship stands with her. If she did pay you back on time, your trust in her would rise a little, and maybe next time you'd trust her with something slightly larger.

Similarly, we can give God opportunities to earn our trust by praying to Him. Ask Him to provide for you. I'm not saying you should test Him by making up irrelevant or extravagant demands just to see what He will do. Be honest with God about your needs and give Him a chance to meet them. If you ask for things you know God wants you to have (like obedience), you will see when He gives them to you that His words are true.

Record your prayers and track how they are answered. Maybe use a prayer journal. I don't write out my prayers each day, but I do make a list of people and situations I'm praying for. That helps me remember the issues I want to pray over. I also make a note about how they're answered. Then I have a reminder to thank God for those answers.

Another way to grow your trust in God is to learn what He has done for other people in various circumstances when they put their trust in

Him. One great source for this type of information is Christians in your community. You likely know some people you could ask about a time when they trusted God and what He did for them.

If you aren't connected with any Christians who have been living in faith for a while, or none you feel comfortable asking about their personal lives, get to know some. Church is a great place to meet other believers and learn their life stories and hear from them how they see God working in their lives. It probably won't happen if you just attend Sunday morning services and head straight back to your life. If you haven't already, start regularly attending a local church. Then get involved in a small group. Most churches offer Bible studies and life groups.

If that kind of intentional relationship building seems too intense for you, try volunteering at your church or another local ministry organization. I have volunteered at my church for many years. I've helped in the nursery, Sunday school, vacation Bible school, and youth group. Through all that, I have made many friends. It's sometimes easier, or at least more comfortable, to get to know a person when you're working on something together. If dealing with kids isn't for you, try greeting, serving coffee, joining the worship team—anything that gives you a chance to meet people in your church and see them on a regular basis.

You can also learn how God worked in the lives of different people by studying the Bible. God wants to be known by His people. That's why He gave us His Word.[53]

---

53   2 Timothy 3:16.

If you've never read the Bible, it's not necessarily recommended that you start at the beginning and read it all the way straight through. The Bible has a lot of amazing stories and great words of wisdom, but there are also parts that can seem kind of dull and some that get pretty confusing if you aren't familiar with the history of the Bible. So my recommendation would be to pick a good story and read it more than once, ideally with a Bible study guide or workbook. If you haven't read the Gospels (Matthew, Mark, Luke, and John) and the book of Acts, I'd say start with those, not necessarily in that order.

When you're ready to move on, read Genesis and Exodus. They tell about God's plan for the world and His people. The books of Ruth and Esther are very good examples of God taking care of His people. They're also interesting dramas I think you'll enjoy.

After several years of reading and studying the Bible regularly, I have learned to always read a section multiple times. Sometimes I read one book of the Bible all the way through, then read it again a few days in a row. Sometimes I read only one section or paragraph a day, three or more times immediately. The first time I read to learn what it's all about and what happens in the story. The next time I make sure I understand who all the characters are and what they represent. (For example, in the parable of the prodigal son, the father represents God, and the older son represents the religious leaders of Jesus's time.[54]) Then I read again and focus on one character at a time, their actions, their motivations, and the lesson I can learn from them.

Joining a Bible study group can be very helpful. Not only will you get to know the other people in your group, you may also help others learn more about the Bible. You can compare your ideas and interpretations,

---

54   Luke 15:11–32.

and others will bring their own background knowledge that can help clear up any parts that cause confusion, allowing you to see things from a new perspective.

Increasing your trust in God can be hindered, though. Your trust in Him is inversely related to your trust in other things and people. The more you put your trust in them, and yourself, the less you'll be able to trust Him. If you think something or someone else is providing what you need, you won't look to God, and you won't give Him the opportunity to demonstrate His faithfulness.

Take some time to think about where you place your trust. Are you relying on people to provide peace, hope, or purpose? Do you put your trust in your money, believing that if you have enough, everything will be okay? Are you trusting the media to tell you who you are and how you're supposed to think and feel? Do you consider yourself to be independent and self-reliant, not wanting to bother God for what you need, thinking you can or should do it all yourself?

If there's anything taking the place of God in your life, confess to Him that you have misplaced your trust and ask for help in trusting Him more. You may not need to cut those other things out entirely. But practice viewing them as less important than God and admit that you still need Him. Even the most trustworthy and reliable person you know is not as wise and powerful as God. Only He is eternal, and He alone will never let you down.

If you have the feeling that there's something other than God that you can't live without, you've put your trust in the wrong place. Whether it's social media, reality TV, news, shopping, chocolate, health supplements, alcohol, or a boyfriend or girlfriend, try spending forty-eight hours without that person or thing. (If it's a person, let them know ahead of time, and specify when you'll get back in contact with them.) Spend some of that free time reading the Bible or practicing your memory verses. (If that's too much for you, tell God you can't do it in your own strength and you need His power to work in you. Give Him this opportunity to earn your trust.)

CHAPTER 7

Yeah, but what do I do when it's too hard to trust God?

If you're facing significant obstacles right now, you may find it impossible to take some of the actions I recommended for increasing your trust in God. What do you do when life makes it extra hard to trust?

Remember that this life isn't all there is. Keeping the right perspective can be hard when this life is all you've ever known. But what you're experiencing now is only part of your existence.

Paul told his students to "fix our eyes not on what is seen, but on what is unseen, since what is seen is temporary, but what is unseen is eternal" (2 Corinthians 4:18). Those words sound deep, but how can we test them to see if they're true?

Have you ever looked forward to something, and it seemed so far away that it would never come, but eventually it did, and then you looked back, and the waiting period seemed brief? Maybe it was a tough school year, and you were struggling just to make it to summer. Perhaps it was as a kid waiting for your birthday or Christmas. Do you remember that feeling of despair, thinking the moment of joy would never come?

When my boyfriend proposed, we decided to plan the wedding for thirteen months later. That would give us plenty of planning and preparation time, and we could reserve the venue we wanted for the day and time of our choosing. I thought a spring wedding and honeymoon would be nice, but one or two months was too little time to plan, so we went for the following spring. It was definitely a smart decision. But there were days when thirteen months felt more like thirteen years. A couple of months before our big day, I thought, *Why did we need so much time? This is taking forever, and I don't know how much longer I can survive the waiting.* Now we've been married for fifteen years, and waiting slightly more than a year seems like no big deal at all. Some of these years have gone by so fast, I wish they would slow down. And those thirteen months of waiting feel like a tiny blip that came and went.

I think that's what this life will feel like someday when we're in heaven. All the struggles and pains we endured will seem brief and minor compared to the joy of eternity with God. Though it's hard for us to imagine what heaven will be like, God sees the whole picture. He knows how everything we go through in this life will lead to blessings in the next.

Sometimes life is really hard. I'm not saying you should never feel sadness or hurt. But when life is painful, that's not because God has given up on you. He is still there, and He is in control. Even when you can't see how this situation could possibly lead to anything good, He sees the bigger picture.

His Word contains promises to us for this life and for heaven. You can trust Him to keep His promises because He is faithful. And His gifts really are best for you. So "lean not on your own understanding" (Proverbs 3:5).

God won't always do what you want or answer your prayers the way you think He should. Sometimes He has a better plan. He knows what would happen if He gave you everything you asked for and whether it would result in something bad. He also knows if it would work out okay but could cause you to miss out on something better. If you acknowledge that, then when life is difficult and you're waiting for circumstances to change, you can trust that the hard days are temporary and better times are ahead. Times that will make all the waiting and enduring worthwhile.

You may have put your trust in God in the past but now find it hard because it seems like God has left or no longer cares about you. You might doubt beliefs you used to hold. I've had a time in my life like that. After a year in which I heard God speak to me and saw what I can only explain as a miracle, I stopped finding answers to my questions. I didn't feel the same connection to God. Because of my previous experiences, I did not give up all faith in the existence of God, but I wondered if the things I had believed about Him were true. I wondered if I could still trust Him.

If you feel the same way, remember that God is faithful and unchanging. We humans are the ones who change. We grow up, we experience different circumstances, we have changing emotions. Everyone has experienced a funky mood caused by lack of sleep, stress from school or work, or no discernible reason at all. Things that normally make you laugh seem irritating, and you become easily frustrated when situations don't go your way. That's why God is more trustworthy than our emotions.

Fickle emotions aside, you may think God no longer hears your prayers because you're not seeing answers. Remember that God does not experience time the same way we do. He may not give you blessings and answers according to your schedule. Because He is all-knowing, He might hold something back until just the right time. He might show up for you when He knows you need to learn something about Him. He has not left you, and He always listens to you. Even now, God is speaking to you and wanting to teach you. But He may speak to you in a way that's different than He has before, and you might need to look for Him in new ways. If you continue to trust in Him, He will reveal Himself to you in time.

After about a year of doubting and questioning, I felt a little inkling of Him wanting me to return to trusting in Him. I realized that to find what I was looking for, I had to start with a small step of faith. As I slowly returned to living my life His way, I gradually gained an understanding that I had to base my trust on who God is, not on how I feel.

Believe it or not, life going really well can be another obstacle to putting your trust in God. I have to admit, there have been times when I felt like I didn't need God. I'm thankful that I've been blessed with a job that provides a sufficient income to meet all my physical needs and still afford lots of stuff that makes my life pleasant and easy. But I have to be careful not to place my trust in that instead of God.

John wrote, "Everything in the world … comes not from the Father but from the world. The world and its desires pass away, but whoever does the will of God lives forever" (1 John 2:16–17). Money and possessions do not truly satisfy, and they will all pass away. Useful things can give us happy feelings. But they break, wear out, get used up. Nothing is dependable like God. I might lose everything I own in less than an hour. Only God cannot be burned up, torn apart by winds, or washed away by floods. Having everything we want and need may give us an illusion of security, but only God is permanent.

Success and achievements may lead you to put too much trust in yourself. It's human nature to take credit for the good things in our lives and blame the bad things on someone else. So we're less likely to acknowledge God when He is blessing us richly. This can be dangerous if we think we have everything figured out. When we depend solely on ourselves, our faith, obedience, wisdom, and peace will decline as we strive to hold it all together. We start out thinking we've got everything under control, but as life has its inevitable ups and downs, we don't turn to God to get us through, but try to muscle through on our own power. A sure-fire way to destroy peace.

If you put your trust in God when life is easy, then when hard times come, you'll be ready to let Him carry you through them. Avoid the temptation to give yourself credit for the gifts God has given you. Humble yourself by admitting that you are not in control.

Have you started a gratitude list yet? In addition to bringing you peace, it can be helpful for increasing your humility. It reminds you to acknowledge God for the gifts He has given you. Even your greatest achievements are dependent on opportunities and skills God has given you. It's okay to feel confident in your own abilities, but keep in mind where those abilities come from.

To retain your trust in God in the good times, practice stepping out in faith by putting yourself into a position that requires you to trust Him to get you through it. Commit to something you sense Him leading you to do but you don't believe you can do on your own. For example, donate money to a charity that's important to you in an amount that leaves almost enough money in your bank account to get you to the next paycheck. Then rely on God to provide for you. Or if you don't have your own means of transportation, volunteer to serve at a place that's too far for you to walk and then pray that God will help you to keep that commitment. Prioritize obedience over your own ability to figure it out. You'll know that you're trusting God if you feel at peace about the situation.

Whatever makes it difficult for you to trust God, you will need His strength to overcome it. The enemy wants to derail you. When you step out in faith, choose obedience, seek wisdom, and find peace, his attacks will come. If you're moving forward on the path God has put before you, you will face temptation to give up. But He will give you the strength to resist it. God's power in you does the work, even the work of trusting Him. So keep asking Him and keep depending on Him to help you trust.

CHAPTER 8

Now what?

I hope I've given you plenty of reasons to believe you can trust God as well as practical ideas to help you increase that trust. A healthy walk with Jesus is made up of trust, faith, and obedience, and it produces wisdom and peace. I hope I've described these properties in such a way that you desire them more than ever. I have faith in you that you can be the kind of Jesus follower you want to be and that you will find a deeper relationship with God.

My story isn't over. I'm not foolish enough to think I'm done learning about how to do life God's way. Recently, God has been teaching me more about humility, faithfulness, and community. I may write a book about those topics someday, but I've got more learning to do first. I don't need to know the whole plan right now.

As long as we are here on this earth, we can continue to learn and improve. As we do, we will find more meaning and satisfaction in our lives. So don't think once you've practiced the strategies I have given you to trust God completely that you will have arrived, that you will be a perfect Christian with no more questions or problems. But you will have confidence as you continue seeking and growing closer to God. You will see Him honor that effort and work in your life.

If you ever need some encouragement and rereading this whole book doesn't seem convenient, put the words of Jeremiah 17:7–8 somewhere you'll see them when you need them:

> Blessed is the one who trusts in the LORD,
>   whose confidence is in him.
> They will be like a tree planted by the water
>   that sends out its roots by the stream.
> It does not fear when heat comes;
>   its leaves are always green.
> It has no worries in a year of drought
>   and never fails to bear fruit.

Every time you see those words, I hope you'll be reminded of the trustworthiness of God.

I am very thankful that God has allowed me and helped me to write this book, and I am so thankful to you for reading it. I have faith that God uses these words to speak to your heart, not because I'm a brilliant writer but because He is a mighty God.

ORDER INFORMATION

To order additional copies of this book, please visit
www.redemption-press.com.
Also available at Christian bookstores, Amazon, and Barnes and Noble.

Milton Keynes UK
Ingram Content Group UK Ltd.
UKHW010638270324
440147UK00003B/95